Microsoft OneDrive

The Microsoft 365 Companion Series

Dr. Patrick Jones

OLYMPUS ACADEMY
PRESS

TABLE OF CONTENTS

TRANSFORMING YOUR WORKFLOW WITH ONEDRIVE

Welcome to the world of Microsoft OneDrive! Imagine having all your important files—documents, photos, presentations, and more—right at your fingertips, no matter where you are. That's what OneDrive is all about. It's a cloud-based storage solution from Microsoft that helps you save, share, and access your files from just about any device with an internet connection. Whether you're at home on your laptop, on the go with your phone, or working from a tablet, OneDrive makes sure your files are ready when you need them.

But OneDrive is more than just a digital storage box. Think of it as the heart of your digital workspace, especially if you're using other Microsoft 365 apps like Word, Excel, and Teams. OneDrive seamlessly connects with these tools, so you can save documents, share files, and work with others without ever needing to juggle multiple programs or email attachments. Imagine starting a report on your laptop, saving it to OneDrive, and then picking up right where you left off on your phone or tablet. And if you need to share it with a teammate, it's as easy as clicking a button.

So, why should you use OneDrive? OneDrive is built for convenience, flexibility, and collaboration. It's designed to keep your files organized, safe, and easy to access, but it also lets you work with others in real time. Need to share a presentation with a colleague? You can send them a link, set permissions for view-only or editing access, and you're good to go. No more worrying about outdated attachments or lost versions—everyone works from the same file.

OneDrive's cloud-based setup also means you don't have to stress about losing important documents if something happens to your computer. Everything is securely stored online, so even if you lose your device, your files are safe. And with features like automatic backups and file versioning, OneDrive is designed to protect your work and give you peace of mind.

This book is here to guide you through the ins and outs of OneDrive. Whether you're brand new to cloud storage or you've used OneDrive a bit and want to dive deeper, this book has you covered. Together, we'll explore everything from setting up your account and uploading files to sharing with others and mastering the features that keep your files organized and secure.

Along the way, you'll also get to know Sarah, who, just like you, is learning how to make the most of OneDrive. Through her journey, you'll see real-life examples of how OneDrive can be used to stay organized, work with teammates, and make everyday tasks easier. Her story is here to show you what's possible and to give you ideas for using OneDrive in ways that fit your life and work.

By the end of this book, you'll know how to:

- **Organize Your Files**: Set up folders, name files clearly, and keep things tidy so you can find what you need in seconds.

- **Collaborate with Ease**: Share files with just a few clicks, set permissions, and work with others in real time.

- **Stay Secure and Protected**: Use OneDrive's backup, version history, and security features to keep your work safe.

OneDrive has the power to transform how you work and keep your digital life organized. Let's dive in and start exploring how OneDrive can help you work smarter, stay connected, and keep everything in its place. Your journey with OneDrive starts now—let's get started!

WHAT IS ONEDRIVE?

Think of OneDrive as your personal, digital storage locker—a safe, flexible space where you can keep all your important files. From documents and photos to presentations and spreadsheets, OneDrive makes it easy to store, access, and share everything you need, no matter where you are. With Microsoft OneDrive, your files live in the cloud, meaning you can get to them from virtually any device with an internet connection. Whether you're at home on your laptop, on the go with your smartphone, or even borrowing someone else's computer, your files are just a few clicks away.

But OneDrive is more than just a storage solution; it's the core of your digital workspace within Microsoft 365. If you're familiar with apps like Word, Excel, and Teams, you've probably seen how closely OneDrive integrates with them. Let's say you're working on a report in Word; saving it to OneDrive lets you pick up right where you left off, even if you switch to a different device. And sharing files becomes a breeze, allowing others to view or edit with just a link—no messy email attachments needed.

Imagine all your files stored in one place, automatically organized and accessible on demand. OneDrive helps you organize and categorize files into folders, making it easy to keep work projects, personal photos, and important documents separate but available whenever you need them. Plus, because it's cloud-based, OneDrive reduces the clutter of hard drives or external storage devices. Everything stays stored in your online account, safe and secure, so you don't have to worry about losing files if your device gets lost or damaged.

Key Benefits of Using OneDrive

OneDrive is designed to make your life easier, especially if you're juggling multiple devices or collaborating with others. Here are a few features that stand out:

- **Access from Anywhere**: No matter where you are or what device you're using, OneDrive lets you access your files. Whether it's your desktop at home, a tablet at work, or your phone while traveling, your files are in reach whenever you need them.

- **Real-Time Collaboration**: When you store files in OneDrive, you can work together on documents in real-time. For example, if you're editing a PowerPoint presentation with a colleague, you can both make changes simultaneously without having to email files back and forth. OneDrive's integration with Microsoft 365 apps like Word, Excel, and Teams makes this seamless.

- **Version History**: Ever wish you could go back to an earlier version of a file? OneDrive's version history feature lets you do just that. This means if you make a mistake, delete something by accident, or simply want to revert to an earlier draft, you can restore previous versions with ease.

- **Secure and Private**: OneDrive comes with strong security features, including encryption and multi-factor authentication, so you know your files are safe.

- **Automatic Syncing Across Devices**: Whenever you save a file in OneDrive, it syncs across all your devices. Make an edit on your desktop, and it will automatically update on your phone or tablet. This means you're always working with the latest version, no matter where you're accessing it from.

OneDrive is more than a storage option; it's a way to simplify your digital life. Gone are the days of cluttered desktops and endless USB drives. With OneDrive, everything is centralized, organized, and always backed up. By offering a single place to store, share, and collaborate on files, OneDrive helps you keep your digital workspace efficient, streamlined, and easy to manage.

WHY USE ONEDRIVE?

So, why should you choose OneDrive as your go-to place for storing and managing files? Simply put, OneDrive makes your life easier by keeping your files safe, organized, and accessible from anywhere. It's more than just storage—it's a tool that adapts to your needs, streamlines your workflow, and makes collaboration a breeze. Here's how OneDrive can make a difference in your daily routine.

1. Access Anytime, Anywhere

With OneDrive, your files are always with you. Imagine having all your documents, photos, and presentations at your fingertips, whether you're working from home, on a business trip, or just grabbing coffee at your favorite cafe. Since OneDrive is cloud-based, you don't have to worry about carrying physical storage or specific devices. You can access everything from any device connected to the internet, making your work truly mobile.

2. Seamless Collaboration with Others

OneDrive shines when it comes to collaboration. Need to work on a project with a colleague or share documents with a group? You can share files in seconds, allowing others to view or even edit them in real time. Forget about multiple versions or long email threads—everyone can work together on the same document, updating it directly in OneDrive. Plus, with integration across Microsoft 365 apps like Word, Excel, and Teams, you can easily share, edit, and communicate about files without leaving your workspace.

3. Safe and Secure File Storage

Security is a top priority, and OneDrive has you covered. From encryption to multi-factor authentication, OneDrive keeps your files protected. It's like having a locked drawer in your digital file cabinet, giving you peace of mind.

4. Automatic Backup and Version History

Ever accidentally delete a file or make changes you wish you hadn't? OneDrive has your back with automatic backups and version history. This means if something goes wrong, you can recover older versions of your files—great for undoing accidental edits or restoring deleted content. It's like having a built-in safety net for your work, so you can focus on creating and organizing without worrying about losing anything important.

5. Effortless Organization and Space Saving

With OneDrive, organization is simple. You can create folders, label files, and even set up a structure that works best for you, so finding what you need is quick and easy. And because your files are stored in the cloud, they're not taking up valuable space on your devices. OneDrive's selective sync feature lets you choose which folders to sync to each device, so you're not bogged down by unnecessary files.

6. Sync Across All Your Devices

OneDrive keeps all your files in sync across your devices, so when you make a change on your laptop, it's automatically updated on your phone or tablet. This ensures you're always working with the most recent version, no matter where you're accessing it from. It's perfect for those moments when you need to make a quick edit on the go or review a document from your phone.

7. A Central Hub for All Your Files in Microsoft 365

OneDrive acts as the central hub for all your files across Microsoft 365. It's designed to work seamlessly with other Microsoft apps, allowing you to save files directly from Word, Excel, or PowerPoint and access them through Teams. This integration makes OneDrive a powerful tool for anyone who uses Microsoft 365, as it ties all your documents and resources together in one accessible place.

OneDrive is more than just a place to store files; it's a way to bring organization, security, and collaboration into your digital life. Whether you're managing personal documents, coordinating with a team, or simply keeping your files safe and accessible, OneDrive gives you the tools to work smarter and stay connected from anywhere. With OneDrive, you're not just storing files—you're creating a system that helps you work, share, and stay organized with ease.

HOW TO GET STARTED

Getting started with OneDrive is easy and can make a huge difference in how you store, share, and access your files. Whether you're new to cloud storage or just setting up OneDrive for the first time, this guide will walk you through the basics to help you get the most out of your OneDrive experience.

1. Access OneDrive on Your Device

OneDrive is available on almost any device, whether you're on a computer, tablet, or smartphone. Here's how to access it:

- **On Your Computer**: If you're using a Windows PC, OneDrive is likely already installed. You can find it by searching for "OneDrive" in the Start menu. On a Mac, you can download the OneDrive app from the App Store.

- **On Your Smartphone or Tablet**: Download the OneDrive app from the Apple App Store (iOS) or Google Play Store (Android). Once installed, open the app to sign in.

2. Sign In with Your Microsoft Account

To start using OneDrive, you'll need to sign in with a Microsoft account. If you already use services like Outlook, Xbox, or Office, you likely already have one. Just enter your username and password, and you're ready to go. If you don't have a Microsoft account, creating one is quick and free on the Microsoft website.

3. Upload Your Files to OneDrive

Once you're signed in, it's time to start uploading files to OneDrive. Here's how:

- **Drag and Drop**: On a computer, simply drag and drop files or folders from your desktop into your OneDrive folder.

- **Use the Upload Button**: In the OneDrive app, you'll see an "Upload" button. Click it, choose the files or folders you want to add, and they'll upload to the cloud.

With your files in OneDrive, you can now access them from any of your devices.

4. Organize Your Files with Folders

Keeping things organized is one of OneDrive's big advantages. Create folders to sort files by project, category, or any system that works best for you.

- **Create a New Folder**: Right-click within OneDrive on your computer or select the "+ New" button on the OneDrive app to create a folder. Name it something descriptive like "Work Projects" or "Family Photos" for easy access.

- **Move Files into Folders**: Just drag your files into the appropriate folders to keep everything tidy. Having a clear folder structure will make finding what you need faster and easier.

5. Set Up OneDrive Sync on Your Devices

One of OneDrive's best features is its ability to sync files across all your devices. Here's how to set it up:

- **On Windows**: Find OneDrive in your taskbar (near the clock in the bottom right corner), right-click the icon, and select "Settings." Under the "Account" tab, click "Choose folders" to pick which files to sync on your device.

- **On Mac**: Open the OneDrive app, sign in, and follow the setup prompts to choose which folders you want to sync.

- **On Mobile**: Open the OneDrive app and go to Settings. Turn on the "Camera Upload" option if you want to automatically save photos and videos from your phone to OneDrive.

Once syncing is set up, OneDrive will automatically keep your files up to date across all devices.

6. Share Files and Collaborate Easily

OneDrive makes it simple to share files with others and work together on documents in real time:

- **Share a File or Folder**: In OneDrive, right-click the file or folder you want to share, then select "Share." You can send a link to specific people, set permissions (like view-only or edit), and even add a password for extra security.

- **Collaborate in Real Time**: If you're working on a Word, Excel, or PowerPoint document, others can edit the document at the same time, making collaboration easier and more efficient.

7. Back Up Important Folders with Known Folder Backup

Known Folder Backup is a OneDrive feature that automatically backs up key folders—like your Desktop, Documents, and Pictures—so they're always safe in the cloud.

- **Turn On Known Folder Backup**: On your PC, open OneDrive, go to "Settings," and select the "Backup" tab. Click "Manage backup" and choose which folders to back up. With this feature, any files you save to these folders will be automatically stored in OneDrive.

8. Find and Restore Older Versions with Version History

If you ever need to recover an older version of a document, OneDrive's version history feature has you covered:

- **Access Version History**: Select the file in OneDrive, choose "Version history," and select the version you want to restore. This is a great safety net if you accidentally make unwanted changes to a file.

Setting up OneDrive is quick and straightforward, and once you're set up, it makes managing and accessing your files a breeze. From uploading and organizing files to sharing with others and syncing across devices, OneDrive helps you stay organized and in control, no matter where you're working from. With these steps, you're ready to take full advantage of all that OneDrive has to offer.

BEST PRACTICES

Now that you've got the basics down, let's dive into some best practices for OneDrive. These tips will help you make the most of OneDrive's features, keeping your files organized, accessible, and secure. Think of this as your guide to mastering OneDrive like a pro!

1. Keep Things Organized from the Start

Imagine OneDrive as a digital filing cabinet. If you just toss all your files in without any organization, things can get messy fast. Set yourself up for success by creating folders and organizing your files right from the start.

- **Create Clear Folder Names**: Think about what makes sense for you. Maybe it's "Work," "Personal," "Projects," or even "2024 Documents." Giving folders clear names will make it easy to find what you need at a glance.

- **Use Subfolders for Extra Clarity**: Sometimes one folder isn't enough. For big projects or lots of files, create subfolders to break things down further. For example, inside "Work," you could have folders like "Reports," "Presentations," and "Client Files."

A little organization up front can save you loads of time later on.

2. Take Advantage of Selective Sync

OneDrive lets you sync files across devices, but syncing everything on every device can take up a lot of space. That's where selective sync comes in.

- **Choose Only What You Need**: Go to your OneDrive settings and pick the folders you actually need to access on each device. This way, you're not filling up your laptop or phone with files you rarely use.

- **Update Your Sync Settings as Needed**: As your projects and priorities change, don't forget to revisit your sync settings. It's easy to adjust which folders sync so you can always access what matters most without clutter.

Selective sync helps you keep devices running smoothly without sacrificing access to important files.

3. Use Version History for Peace of Mind

We've all been there: you accidentally overwrite a file or delete something important. Luckily, OneDrive has your back with version history.

- **Access Older Versions Easily**: If you need to go back to a previous version, just select the file in OneDrive and choose "Version history." You can restore an older version with a click, so no worries about accidental edits.

- **Keep Track of Changes on Shared Files**: If you're working on a document with others, version history is a lifesaver. You can see who made changes and when, so you're always in the loop.

Version history is like an "undo" button for your OneDrive files. Don't hesitate to use it!

4. Make Sharing Simple but Secure

Sharing files on OneDrive is super convenient, but it's important to keep security in mind—especially for sensitive documents.

- **Use "Specific People" Sharing for Control**: When you share a file, choose "Specific People" rather than "Anyone with the link." This limits access to only the people you specify, keeping your files more secure.

- **Set Permissions Wisely**: If someone only needs to view a file, set it to "View Only." If they need to collaborate, you can give them editing permissions, but this added layer of control helps prevent accidental changes.

- **Consider Adding a Password for Extra Security**: For highly sensitive files, you can add a password to shared links. This gives you extra peace of mind, especially if you're sharing outside your organization.

Sharing is easy and safe when you use the right permissions—keep it secure, and you're good to go.

5. Keep Your OneDrive Clean and Updated

OneDrive can get cluttered over time if you're constantly adding files and rarely cleaning up. Make it a habit to do a little digital housekeeping now and then.

- **Delete Files You No Longer Need**: Old files, drafts, or duplicates can pile up quickly. Every now and then, go through your folders and remove anything you don't need.

- **Archive Older Projects**: If you have finished projects or files you want to keep but don't need regularly, move them to a dedicated "Archive" folder. This way, you have access to them without them getting in the way of current work.

A tidy OneDrive is a happy OneDrive. Regular clean-up makes finding what you need easier and keeps your digital space in order.

6. Use Offline Access for On-the-Go Productivity

OneDrive is great for cloud storage, but there are times when you might not have internet access—like when you're on a plane or in a remote location.

- **Download Important Files for Offline Use**: For files you know you'll need when you're offline, download them in advance. Right-click on the file and choose "Make available offline" to ensure you can access it without internet.

- **Set Up Offline Access on Mobile**: In the OneDrive mobile app, you can mark files or folders to be available offline. This is perfect for keeping key documents handy, even when you're out and about.

Offline access ensures you're never stranded without the files you need.

7. Backup Your Desktop, Documents, and Pictures Folders

OneDrive's Known Folder Backup lets you automatically back up the files from your Desktop, Documents, and Pictures folders to the cloud, keeping them safe and accessible.

- **Turn on Known Folder Backup**: In OneDrive settings, go to the Backup tab and enable Known Folder Backup. This keeps your most-used folders backed up, protecting them from accidental deletion or device loss.

- **Easily Recover Files**: With this setup, you can access your Desktop, Documents, and Pictures from any device, anytime. It's also great for peace of mind if you ever switch computers.

Known Folder Backup is like having an automatic safety net for your files. It's one less thing to worry about.

By following these best practices, you'll keep your OneDrive organized, secure, and always ready to support your work and personal projects. From using selective sync to keeping files in the Personal Vault, these tips help you make the most of OneDrive's features and avoid common pitfalls. With OneDrive, you've got the tools to work smarter, collaborate easier, and keep your digital life running smoothly—no matter where you are.

TIPS AND TRICKS

Ready to get more out of OneDrive? Here are some practical tips and clever tricks to help you work faster, stay organized, and take full advantage of OneDrive's features. Whether you're looking to save space, speed up your workflow, or boost security, these tips will keep you moving forward with ease.

1. Use File On-Demand to Save Space on Your Device

If you're tight on storage, OneDrive's Files On-Demand feature can help. It shows all your files in File Explorer, but only downloads them when you need them. This way, you can access everything without filling up your hard drive.

- **Turn On Files On-Demand**: Go to OneDrive settings and enable Files On-Demand. You'll see little cloud icons for files stored only in the cloud and a checkmark for files available offline.

- **Download as Needed**: If you need a file offline, right-click it and choose "Always keep on this device." Otherwise, leave it online-only to save space.

2. Use Search to Find Files Quickly

With OneDrive, you don't have to dig through folders to find what you're looking for. The Search feature is a huge timesaver, especially if you have a lot of files.

- **Use Keywords**: Type in keywords related to the file name, contents, or even file type to narrow down your search quickly.

- **Filter by Type or Date**: Once you've searched, use filters to refine results by file type (like Word documents, PDFs) or date modified. This makes locating specific files even faster.

17

3. Add Files to OneDrive from Any App

You don't have to open OneDrive every time you want to save something there. Most apps let you save files directly to OneDrive, making it easy to keep everything in one place.

- **Choose OneDrive as Your Save Location**: When saving a document or file, choose your OneDrive folder as the location. This works in Microsoft apps like Word, Excel, and PowerPoint, but also in many other applications.

- **Quickly Upload Screenshots and Photos**: If you're working on a mobile device, use the OneDrive app's built-in camera feature to save photos directly to your OneDrive. It's perfect for capturing receipts, notes, or important images on the go.

4. Quickly Access Recently Used Files

Sometimes you just need to jump back into a document you were recently working on. OneDrive makes this easy with its Recent Files feature.

- **Check Recent Files**: In OneDrive (desktop or mobile), go to the "Recent" tab to see your latest files. It's especially handy if you're switching devices and want to pick up where you left off.

- **Use in Microsoft 365 Apps**: In apps like Word or Excel, you'll also find a list of recent documents linked to your OneDrive account, making it easy to access frequently used files without extra steps.

5. Use Camera Upload to Automatically Save Photos

OneDrive's mobile app has a Camera Upload feature that can automatically save photos and videos you take with your phone.

- **Enable Camera Upload**: Open the OneDrive app on your phone, go to Settings, and turn on Camera Upload. Your photos and videos will automatically upload to your OneDrive, keeping them safe and freeing up space on your phone.

- **Organize Photos into Folders**: You can set OneDrive to organize your photos by date or create custom folders for events. This makes it easy to find photos later.

6. Add a Shortcut to Shared Folders for Easy Access

If someone has shared a OneDrive folder with you, you can add a shortcut to it in your OneDrive, making it easier to find.

- **Add to My Files**: When viewing a shared folder, click "Add to My Files." This places the folder in your OneDrive directory, so you can access it just like any other folder without hunting for shared links.

7. Annotate PDFs Directly in OneDrive (Mobile)

Need to mark up a PDF quickly? The OneDrive mobile app lets you **annotate PDFs** right in the app.

- **Open PDF in OneDrive**: Tap a PDF in OneDrive's mobile app, and you'll see an option to annotate.

- **Highlight, Draw, or Add Text**: Use the built-in tools to highlight important parts, draw shapes, or add notes. This feature is great for reviewing documents or signing PDFs on the go.

8. Restore Files from the OneDrive Recycle Bin

Accidentally deleted a file? Don't panic! OneDrive keeps deleted files in its Recycle Bin for a period of time, so you can easily restore them.

- **Go to the Recycle Bin**: Open OneDrive and select "Recycle Bin" in the sidebar. Here, you'll find recently deleted files.

- **Restore with a Click**: Select the files you want to recover, and click "Restore." They'll go back to their original locations.

9. Share Links with Expiry Dates for Extra Security

When sharing files, sometimes you want the access to be temporary. OneDrive lets you add expiry dates to shared links, so they'll automatically expire after a set period.

- **Set an Expiry Date**: When sharing a file, click on the link settings and choose an expiry date. This is great for sensitive files or time-limited projects, ensuring your files aren't accessible forever.

- **Remove Access Anytime**: If you want to revoke access to a shared link sooner, you can do that, too. Just go back to the file's sharing settings and remove the link.

10. Collaborate Smoothly by Leaving Comments on Files

OneDrive allows you to add comments to files, making it easier to leave feedback or notes for collaborators.

- **Add Comments**: Right-click on a file, choose "Open in Word Online" (or another app), and leave a comment. Comments appear in real-time, so collaborators can see and respond instantly.

- **Review Comments Easily**: In Microsoft 365 apps, comments are displayed in a side panel, so they don't clutter the main document.

11. Use Known Folder Move for Automatic Backup

Known Folder Move is a OneDrive feature that backs up key folders—like Desktop, Documents, and Pictures—directly to OneDrive.

- **Enable Known Folder Move**: In OneDrive settings, find the Backup tab and enable Known Folder Move. This ensures these important folders are always backed up and accessible from other devices.

- **Recover Easily on a New Device**: With this setup, moving to a new computer is easy—just log in to OneDrive, and your Desktop, Documents, and Pictures will be right where you left them.

With these tips and tricks, OneDrive becomes more than just a place to store files. It's a powerful tool for staying organized, productive, and secure, no matter where you're working from. Try out these tricks to save time, keep your files safe, and get the most out of everything OneDrive has to offer. Once you get the hang of it, you'll wonder how you ever managed without these helpful features.

COPILOT IN ONEDRIVE: UNLOCKING NEW LEVELS OF PRODUCTIVITY

Imagine having an assistant that not only organizes your files but also helps you find them faster, automates tasks, and offers intelligent suggestions—all within your OneDrive workspace. This is the promise of Microsoft Copilot in OneDrive, a cutting-edge AI-driven feature designed to make your file management smarter and your workflow more efficient. In this chapter, we'll explore how Copilot enhances your OneDrive experience, with practical examples to help you get the most out of this powerful tool.

Copilot is more than just an AI assistant—it's a game-changer for how you interact with your files in OneDrive. By leveraging artificial intelligence and contextual awareness, Copilot helps you:

- Organize and manage files more effectively.

- Search for documents and data with greater precision.

- Automate repetitive tasks like sharing or renaming files.

- Gain insights from the content stored in your OneDrive.

Think of Copilot as your personal assistant, working in the background to simplify file management while freeing you to focus on more important tasks.

Let's look at some specific ways Copilot can enhance your OneDrive experience:

1. Smarter File Organization

One of Copilot's key strengths is its ability to help you organize your files intelligently. If your OneDrive is a maze of folders and filenames, Copilot can suggest ways to streamline it.

- **Example**: Sarah has a cluttered OneDrive filled with unorganized client files. By asking Copilot, "Can you organize my files by project?" she receives suggestions for creating folders and sorting files into categories like "Completed Projects," "Active Clients," and "Archived Work."
- **Pro Tip**: Use prompts like "Show me redundant or duplicate files" to declutter your storage.

2. Advanced Search and Contextual Retrieval

Finding the right file in a sea of documents can be time-consuming, but Copilot transforms OneDrive's search capabilities into a more intuitive and efficient process.

- **Example**: Sarah remembers uploading a proposal last month but can't recall the filename. She types, "Find the proposal I shared with Marketing in March," and Copilot quickly locates the document based on her sharing history and contextual details.
- **Pro Tip**: Use natural language prompts, like "Find the Excel file I updated last week," for even faster results.

3. Automating Routine Tasks

Copilot takes care of repetitive tasks, saving you time and effort. Whether it's renaming files, sharing them with colleagues, or setting permissions, Copilot simplifies these processes.

- **Example**: Sarah needs to share a folder of campaign assets with her design team. Instead of manually setting permissions for each file, she asks Copilot, "Share this folder with the Design team and give them edit access." Within seconds, the task is complete.
- **Pro Tip**: Automate file permissions for recurring projects by using Copilot prompts like "Apply the same sharing settings as this folder."

4. Summarizing and Extracting Key Information

With Copilot, you can go beyond just storing files to extracting valuable insights from them. Copilot can summarize document content, highlight important points, or pull out data from within files.

- **Example**: Sarah has a folder filled with meeting minutes and client reports. She asks Copilot, "Summarize the key takeaways from all the files in this folder," and receives a concise overview that saves her hours of manual review.

- **Pro Tip**: Use prompts like "Find the deadlines mentioned in these documents" to quickly gather actionable insights.

5. Enhanced Collaboration

OneDrive is a powerful tool for collaboration, and Copilot takes it to the next level by helping you manage shared files more effectively.

- **Example**: Sarah wants to track updates on a shared folder her team is using for a new campaign. She asks Copilot, "What changes have been made to the Campaign folder this week?" and receives a summary of edits and uploads by her teammates.

- **Pro Tip**: Combine Copilot with Teams to track collaborative efforts seamlessly across both platforms.

6. Insights for Better Storage Management

Running low on OneDrive storage? Copilot can analyze your files and recommend ways to free up space.

- **Example**: Sarah's OneDrive is nearing its storage limit. She asks Copilot, "Identify large or unused files I can delete," and receives a report of outdated files and large media items she no longer needs.

- **Pro Tip**: Schedule Copilot to run storage checks monthly to stay ahead of space issues.

Getting started with Copilot is easy. Here's how:

1. **Activate Copilot**: Look for the Copilot icon in your OneDrive interface, or access it via a keyboard shortcut.

2. **Ask for Assistance**: Type or speak your request using natural language. Be as specific as possible to get tailored results.

3. **Refine as Needed**: If the output isn't quite right, refine your prompt or ask follow-up questions to clarify.

4. **Integrate Across Microsoft 365**: Use Copilot in conjunction with other apps like Word, Excel, or Teams to unlock even more functionality.

To make the most of Copilot, keep these tips in mind:

- Be clear and specific in your prompts to ensure accurate results.
- Use Copilot to automate repetitive tasks, freeing up time for more important work.
- Regularly review and act on Copilot's suggestions to keep your OneDrive organized and efficient.

Copilot isn't just a tool—it's a partner in productivity. By simplifying file management, enhancing search capabilities, and automating routine tasks, Copilot allows you to focus on what truly matters. Whether you're a professional managing large projects or a student organizing class materials, Copilot in OneDrive is here to make your work easier and more effective.

OneDrive, enhanced with Copilot, is a powerful tool in its own right, but it shines even brighter as part of the Microsoft 365 ecosystem. In the final chapter, we'll explore how tools like OneDrive connect with other apps to create a seamless workflow that supports your productivity, creativity, and collaboration. Let's continue the journey together!

COMMON PITFALLS AND HOW TO AVOID THEM

Like any powerful tool, OneDrive can come with a few hiccups if you're not aware of the best ways to use it. Here are some common mistakes users encounter in OneDrive, along with simple solutions to help you sidestep them and keep things running smoothly. Let's make sure OneDrive works for you, not against you!

1. Accidental Sharing with the Wrong People

Pitfall:

It's easy to accidentally share files with more people than intended. This usually happens when choosing the wrong sharing settings or using a link that allows access to "Anyone with the link."

How to Avoid It:

- **Use "Specific People" Sharing**: When you share a file, choose "Specific People" to ensure only those individuals can access it.

- **Double-Check Permissions**: Take an extra second to confirm permissions before sharing. You can set links to be "View Only" or "Edit," so choose what's appropriate.

- **Review Shared Files Regularly**: Go to the "Shared" view in OneDrive to see everything you've shared. This quick checkup lets you remove access for anyone who no longer needs it.

A little extra caution can keep your files in the right hands!

2. Letting Files Get Disorganized

Pitfall:
Dumping everything into OneDrive without a system can lead to chaos, making it hard to find what you need.

How to Avoid It:

- **Create a Folder Structure**: Set up folders with names that make sense to you, like "Work," "Personal," or "2024 Projects." Within these, you can create subfolders as needed.

- **Use Descriptive Names**: Name files and folders with clear, specific labels, like "Client_Project_Report_March2024" rather than something vague.

- **Declutter Regularly**: Schedule a quick cleanup every month or so. Delete outdated files and organize any loose items. This keeps your OneDrive tidy and easy to navigate.

Staying organized from the start (and maintaining it) will save you time and frustration later.

3. Running Out of Storage Space

Pitfall:
OneDrive storage can fill up quickly, especially if you're storing lots of high-resolution photos or large project files.

How to Avoid It:

- **Use Files On-Demand**: With Files On-Demand, you can keep files stored in the cloud without taking up space on your device.

- **Check Storage Usage**: OneDrive shows your storage usage in settings, so you can easily see if you're getting close to your limit.

- **Delete or Archive Unnecessary Files**: Every so often, go through and delete files you don't need or move old projects to an "Archive" folder. Freeing up space makes room for what's important.

These small actions can help you make the most of your OneDrive storage.

4. Losing Files Due to Accidental Deletion

Pitfall:
Deleting files by accident happens to the best of us, and it can be a big headache if it's something important.

How to Avoid It:

- **Check the Recycle Bin**: OneDrive's Recycle Bin keeps deleted files for 30 days (or longer on some plans), so you can recover accidentally deleted files with a few clicks.

- **Turn on Version History**: Version history lets you revert to earlier versions of a file if you make a change you didn't mean to. It's like an extra safety net.

- **Use Known Folder Backup**: Enable Known Folder Backup to automatically back up important folders like Desktop, Documents, and Pictures, so your key files are always protected.

These backup features offer peace of mind, so don't hesitate to use them.

5. Confusing Sync Settings Across Devices

Pitfall:
If you're syncing everything across all your devices, you might end up with storage issues or slowdowns, especially on mobile.

How to Avoid It:

- **Use Selective Sync**: Choose only the folders you really need on each device. This saves space and ensures each device has what's relevant.

- **Adjust Sync Settings as Needed**: If your needs change, update your sync preferences in OneDrive's settings. You can add or remove folders anytime.

- **Resolve Sync Conflicts Quickly**: If you see a conflict icon on a file, open the "View sync problems" menu to address it. Choosing the right version or renaming a duplicate file can prevent issues from spreading.

Selective sync keeps your devices clutter-free and running smoothly.

6. Overlooking Security Settings

Pitfall:
Not taking advantage of OneDrive's security features can leave sensitive files vulnerable to unauthorized access.

How to Avoid It:

- **Set Permissions Thoughtfully**: Limit access when sharing by setting files to "View Only" if people don't need editing rights. This keeps your files safer.

- **Password Protect Links**: When sharing sensitive info, add a password to the link. This simple step adds extra security, especially when sharing outside your organization.

These settings ensure your files are protected, even when you're sharing.

7. Relying on OneDrive as Your Only Backup Solution

Pitfall:
While OneDrive is a great backup tool, relying on it alone could be risky if there's a sync error or an accidental deletion.

How to Avoid It:

- **Set Up an Additional Backup**: For your most important files, keep an extra backup on an external hard drive or secondary cloud service.

- **Enable Known Folder Backup**: This feature backs up files in your Desktop, Documents, and Pictures folders automatically, so you always have an extra copy of these critical files.

- **Regularly Review Backups**: Check that your essential files are backed up to multiple locations and update them as needed.

A second backup adds an extra layer of protection, so you're always covered.

8. Forgetting to Clean Up Shared Files

Pitfall:
Leaving old shared files and links active can lead to unnecessary clutter and potential privacy risks.

How to Avoid It:

- **Review Shared Links Regularly**: Go to the "Shared" view in OneDrive and check the links you've shared. Remove access for files that are no longer relevant.

- **Set Expiry Dates for Links**: For temporary projects, add an expiration date to shared links. This way, access automatically ends after a set period.

- **Remove Access for Completed Projects**: Once a project wraps up, remove sharing permissions for related files to keep things secure.

Keeping track of shared files and links ensures privacy and reduces clutter.

By avoiding these common pitfalls, you'll make the most of OneDrive and enjoy a smoother, more secure experience. From organizing files and using selective sync to checking permissions and setting up backups, these best practices keep your OneDrive account running like a well-oiled machine. Remember, a little extra care goes a long way in keeping your files safe, organized, and easy to access whenever you need them.

SARAH'S STRUGGLE WITH CLUTTERED FILES

Sarah sat at her cluttered desk, staring at the screen in frustration. Another week, another dozen versions of the same report scattered across her desktop and inbox. As a project manager, Sarah loved her work, but keeping up with the constant flow of documents from her team was overwhelming. Each project came with new documents, revisions, approvals, and more emails than she could handle. Despite her best efforts, her desktop had become a digital mess, and every morning she braced herself for the search-and-sort routine to find the latest file versions.

Just as she was considering printing everything out to escape the digital clutter, her colleague Michael noticed her frustration. "You should try OneDrive," he suggested, his voice light but with a hint of authority.

Sarah had heard of OneDrive, of course, but she hadn't thought to use it. She had tried organizing her files in folders, even color-coding, but it hadn't helped much. "Isn't it just a storage app?" she asked, skeptical but intrigued.

Michael shook his head. "It's so much more than that. Think of it as a workspace, a place to organize, share, and collaborate in real time. It might just save you from all… this." He gestured to her chaotic desktop.

Sarah wasn't sure if she was ready to embrace a new tool, but that evening, she decided to give it a try. Logging into OneDrive felt like stepping into a blank slate, clean and uncluttered—a sharp contrast to her desktop. As she started adding files, she felt a cautious excitement. Each document and folder went into a dedicated space, easy to reach, easy to search. It wasn't long before she wondered if Michael was right.

The next morning, Sarah opened OneDrive on her laptop and started organizing her projects. It felt good to finally have a place where everything made sense. She created folders for each project, uploaded relevant files, and named each document in a way that made sense. The chaotic shuffling between emails and desktop icons was slowly being replaced with a clear, manageable structure.

Soon, Sarah began discovering OneDrive's more advanced features. She learned she could share files with her team with just a link, setting permissions to ensure everyone had the right access. Real-time collaboration became a reality, allowing her team to work on the same document without dozens of email attachments. She no longer had to keep track of who had the latest version—OneDrive did it for her.

But the real game-changer was version history. On a stressful day, she accidentally overwrote a key document with a few incorrect changes. Panic set in until she remembered Michael mentioning that OneDrive saved previous versions. With a quick right-click, she found the version history, restored the original file, and felt an immense wave of relief. Her work was safe, even from her own mistakes.

Of course, Sarah's journey wasn't without challenges. At first, she struggled to break her habit of saving files to her desktop. She would sometimes find herself searching for a document in the wrong place, forgetting it was safely stored in OneDrive. But each small misstep reminded her of the benefits of the cloud, and with time, her habits began to change. She also faced a minor sync issue on her tablet, but with a bit of troubleshooting and some guidance from online tutorials, she had it working smoothly.

As Sarah grew more comfortable with OneDrive, she found herself spending less time on the mundane tasks of locating, sorting, and sharing files. The time she once spent searching was now used for refining her reports, brainstorming ideas, and supporting her team. OneDrive became more than just a tool; it was her personal assistant, keeping everything within reach without the hassle.

Sarah began exploring other productivity hacks within OneDrive. She started using the "Files On-Demand" feature, which allowed her to keep large files in the cloud without taking up space on her device. She set up automatic backups for important documents, using OneDrive as a safety net for her most valuable work.

Just when Sarah thought she had mastered OneDrive, a new challenge arose. Preparing for an important client presentation, she logged into OneDrive to pull up her presentation file—but it wasn't there. Her heart skipped a beat as she realized she had moved the file without remembering where she put it. The clock was ticking, and her team was depending on her to have everything ready. With the skills she'd learned, Sarah had to rely on OneDrive's search and version history features to track down her presentation in time for the meeting.

UNDERSTANDING THE POWER OF ONEDRIVE

We explored Microsoft OneDrive in depth, from the foundational features to practical tips and best practices that can transform how you store, organize, and share your files. OneDrive is more than a storage solution; it's a tool that adapts to your needs, keeping your digital workspace organized and secure, while offering seamless access from anywhere.

Here's a recap of what we covered:

- **What OneDrive Is**: A flexible, cloud-based hub for storing, accessing, and sharing files, integrated with the entire Microsoft 365 suite.

- **Why Use OneDrive**: From easy file sharing and collaboration to reliable backups and secure access, OneDrive provides features designed to simplify and protect your work.

- **How to Get Started**: Setting up OneDrive on your devices, organizing your files, and enabling key features like sync and backup.

- **Best Practices**: Simple strategies like using selective sync, creating a clear folder structure, and keeping files up to date ensure your OneDrive remains efficient and easy to navigate.

- **Tips and Tricks**: From using Files On-Demand to taking advantage of version history, we explored practical ways to get the most out of OneDrive.

- **Avoiding Common Pitfalls**: Staying aware of potential issues like accidental sharing and storage limits can help you avoid disruptions and stay on track.

Through Sarah's story, we saw how OneDrive can become more than just a place to save files. At first, Sarah approached OneDrive as simply a convenient storage tool. But as she explored its capabilities, she realized it could do much more—helping her streamline her workflow, stay organized, and collaborate more effectively. Each feature she discovered, from version history to shared folder access, supported her in managing projects, keeping her files secure, and ensuring she always had access to the latest versions.

Sarah's journey mirrors the learning path for anyone new to OneDrive. Just like her, you may have started with the basics, but with each step, you've gained confidence and found new ways to make OneDrive work for you. By applying what you've learned, you can turn OneDrive into a central, reliable part of your digital workspace, helping you accomplish tasks with greater efficiency and control.

This knowledge not only prepares you to get the most out of OneDrive but also opens the door to exploring other Microsoft 365 tools with the same curiosity and confidence. Just as OneDrive has supported Sarah's projects, it can support yours—making your workflow more streamlined, collaborative, and secure.

With this foundation, you're ready to dive deeper into the potential of Microsoft 365, discovering new ways to enhance your work and reach your goals.

EMBRACING THE POWER OF ONEDRIVE AND BEYOND

As we reach the end of our journey with Microsoft OneDrive, it's clear how much a single tool can impact the way we work, organize, and collaborate. OneDrive offers more than just storage; it's a platform that helps us stay connected, access our files anywhere, and work with others seamlessly. By learning to harness OneDrive's capabilities, you've gained control over your digital workspace, transforming how you manage files, protect your information, and collaborate with ease.

With OneDrive, your files are organized, secure, and always within reach, whether you're working from your desktop, laptop, or mobile device. You've explored ways to structure folders for clarity, use sharing settings for secure collaboration, and access advanced features like file versioning and backups. These skills empower you to approach projects with confidence and precision, knowing your files are protected and your workflow is streamlined.

But this journey with Microsoft 365 doesn't end here. OneDrive is just one tool in a suite designed to empower you in all aspects of work and productivity. Imagine being able to take the same efficiency, flexibility, and ease you've mastered with OneDrive and apply it across other Microsoft 365 apps, like Word for document creation, Excel for data management, Teams for seamless communication, and Planner for task management.

Each app in Microsoft 365 brings its own set of features and unique value, all designed to help you work better, smarter, and more connected with your team or clients. Mastering each tool opens new possibilities in your workflow and equips you with the knowledge to tackle tasks more creatively and efficiently.

By continuing your journey into the full Microsoft 365 suite, you're not just learning new skills—you're transforming the way you work and engage with technology. Every app you explore adds another layer to your productivity and enhances your ability to communicate, organize, and create. Just as you've seen with OneDrive, these tools go beyond their primary functions, opening doors to new ways of thinking, collaborating, and achieving your goals.

So, as you move forward, remember that each app in Microsoft 365 is an opportunity to learn, grow, and become even more adept at managing your digital world. With each step, you're not only learning software; you're building a foundation that empowers you to work confidently, creatively, and efficiently in today's dynamic environment.

Thank you for taking this journey with OneDrive. Your next adventure in Microsoft 365 awaits—let's continue to unlock the possibilities together.